Thai Cooking for Everyone

Learn the Thai Way to Cooking and Surprise Your
Guests with Amazing Recipes

Tim Singhapat.

Table of contents

THAI–STYLE BEAN SPROUTS AND SNAP PEAS

Ingredients:

- ½ pound sugar snap peas, trimmed

- 1 (1-inch) piece ginger, peeled and minced
- Pinch of white pepper 1 pound bean sprouts, washed meticulously and trimmed if required

- 1 small onion, thinly cut

- 1 tablespoon soy sauce

- 2 tablespoons vegetable oil

- Salt and sugar to taste

Directions:

1. Heat the vegetable oil on moderate to high heat in a big frying pan.

2. Put in the onion and the ginger and sauté for a minute.

3. Mix in the white pepper and the soy sauce.

4. Put in the sugar snap peas and cook, stirring continuously, for a minute.

5. Put in the bean sprouts and cook for 1 more minute while stirring continuously.

6. Put in up to ½ teaspoon of salt and a big pinch of sugar to adjust the balance of the sauce. Serve instantly.

Yield: Servings 4–6

THAI-STYLE FRIED OKRA

Ingredients:

- ½ cup tapioca flour

- ½ cup water

- 1 cup all-purpose flour

- 1 cup vegetable oil

- 1 pound small okra, trimmed

- 1 recipe chili dipping sauce of your choice

- 1 teaspoon baking powder

Directions:

1. In a moderate-sized-sized mixing container, mix the flours, the baking soda, and water to make a batter. Put in the okra pieces.
2. Heat the vegetable oil in a frying pan or wok using high heat. (It must be hot enough that a test piece of batter puffs up instantly.)

3. Put in the battered okra, a few at a time, and fry until golden.

4. Using a slotted spoon, remove the okra to paper towels to drain.

5. Serve hot with your favorite chili dipping sauce.

Yield: Approximately 20

TROPICAL VEGETABLES

Ingredients:

- ½ cup coconut milk

- 1 shallot, minced

- 1 tablespoon fish sauce

- 1 tablespoon Red Curry Paste (Page 17)

- 1 tablespoon sesame seeds

- 1 tablespoon Tamarind Concentrate (Page 20)

- 1 teaspoon vegetable oil

- 1 yellow or red bell pepper, seeded and julienned

- 2 cups bamboo shoots

- 2 cups bean sprouts

- 2 tablespoons brown sugar

- 2½ cups baby spinach leaves

- 2½ cups green beans, trimmed and slice into 1-inch lengths

Directions:

1. To make the sauce, heat the vegetable oil in a small sauté pan on moderate to high. Put in the minced shallot and fry until golden. Move the fried shallot to paper towels to drain.
2. Using a mortar and pestle, crush half of the sesame seeds and half of the fried shallots together; set aside.

3. In a small deep cooking pan, mix the Red Curry Paste (Page 17) and the coconut milk, and bring to a simmer on moderate to low heat. Put in the tamarind, brown sugar, fish sauce, and the reserved sesame seed? shallot mixture. Decrease the heat to low and keep warm.

4. Bring a big deep cooking pan of water to its boiling point. Put in the green beans, the bell pepper pieces, and the bamboo shoots to the water and blanch for half a minute to one minute or until done to your preference. Using a slotted spoon, remove the vegetables from the water to a colander to drain.

5. Allow the water return to boiling and put in the spinach leaves and the bean sprouts.

Instantly remove them from the water to drain.

6. Toss all of the vegetables together.

7. To serve, put the vegetables in the middle of a serving plate. Pour some of the sauce over the vegetables. Pass additional sauce separately.

Yield: Servings 8–10

VEGETABLES POACHED IN COCONUT MILK

Ingredients:

- ½ cup cut mushrooms

- ½ cup long beans or green beans, broken
- into two-inch pieces ½ cup peas

- ½ teaspoon cut kaffir lime leaves

- 1 cup coconut milk

- 1 cup shredded cabbage

- 1 shallot, finely chopped

- 1 tablespoon brown sugar

- 1 tablespoon green peppercorns

- 1 tablespoon soy sauce

    1 tablespoon Thai chilies,
    seeded and finely cut Rice,
- cooked in accordance with
- package directions

Directions:

1. In a deep cooking pan bring the coconut milk to a gentle simmer moderate heat. Mix in the shallots, soy sauce, brown sugar, green peppercorn pouch, and lime leaves. Simmer for 1 until aromatic.

2. Put in the green beans, mushrooms, and cabbage, and return simmer. Cook for five to ten minutes or until soft.

3. Put in the peas and cook 1 more minute. Take away the pouch before you serve over rice.

Yield: Servings 2–4

VEGETARIAN STIR-FRY

Ingredients:

- ¼ cup asparagus tips

- ¼ cup bean sprouts

- ¼ cup bite-sized pieces bell pepper

- ¼ cup broccoli florets

- ¼ cup cauliflower florets

- ¼ cup cut mushrooms

- ¼ cup snow peas

- ¼ cup thinly cut celery

- ¼ cup water chestnuts

- 1 small onion, cut

- 1 tablespoon cornstarch, dissolved in a little water

- 1-2 tablespoons vegetable oil

- 2 cups bite-sized tofu pieces

- 2 tablespoons dark sweet soy sauce

- 2 tablespoons grated ginger

- 2 tablespoons minced garlic

- 4 tablespoons seeded and cut Thai chilies

- 4 tablespoons soy sauce

- Rice, cooked in accordance with package directions

Directions:

1. Heat 1 tablespoon of oil in a big frying pan or wok over moderate-heat. Put in the tofu and sauté until a golden-brown colour is achieved. Move paper towels to drain.

2. Put in additional oil to the frying pan if required, and stir-fry the ginger, and chilies to release their fragrance, approximately 2 to Mix in the soy sauces and raise the heat to high.

3. Put in the reserved tofu and all the vegetables apart from the bean stir-fry for a minute.

4. Put in the cornstarch mixture and stir-fry for one more minute or until the vegetables are

just thoroughly cooked and the sauce has thickened somewhat.

5. Put in the bean sprouts, stirring for a short period of time to warm them.

6. Serve over rice.

Yield: Servings 4–6 as a main course

BROCCOLI NOODLES WITH GARLIC AND SOY

Ingredients:

- 1 pound broccoli, trimmed into bite-sized florets

- 1 tablespoon sugar

- 1 tablespoon sweet soy sauce

- 1–2 tablespoons vegetable oil

- 16 ounces rice noodles

- 2 cloves garlic, minced

- 2 tablespoons soy sauce

- Fish sauce

- Hot sauce

- Lime wedges

Directions:

1. Bring a pot of water to boil using high heat. Drop in the broccoli and blanch until soft-

crisp or to your preference. Drain and save for later.

2. Soak the rice noodles in hot water until soft, approximately ten minutes.

3. In a big sauté pan, heat the vegetable oil on medium. Put in the garlic and stir-fry until golden. Put in the soy sauces and the sugar, stirring until the sugar has thoroughly blended.

4. Put in the reserved noodles, tossing until thoroughly coated with the sauce. Put in the broccoli and toss to coat.

5. Serve instantly with hot sauce, fish sauce, and lime wedges on the side.

Yield: Servings 2–4

CHIANG MAI CURRIED NOODLES

Ingredients:

- ¼ pound ground pork

- ½ cup coconut milk

- 1 tablespoon chopped garlic

- 1 tablespoon curry powder Pinch of turmeric powder

- 1 tablespoon Red Curry Paste (Page 17)

- 1 teaspoon lime juice

- 2 tablespoons fish sauce Pinch of sugar

- 4 ounces rice noodles, soaked in water for twenty minutes to half an hour or until tender Lime wedges, for decoration

Directions:

1. Heat the coconut milk in a wok or heavy frying pan on moderate heat. Mix in the curry paste and cook until aromatic and a thin film of oil separates out.

2. Put in the garlic and cook for approximately half a minute. Put in the remainingingredients apart from the pork, noodles, and limes, and cook until the sauce thickens slightly, stirring continuously.

3. Put in the pork and continue to stir until the meat is thoroughly cooked. Decrease the heat and keep the sauce warm.
4. Bring a pan of water to a rolling boil. Put the noodles in a wire basket or strainer and immerse the noodles in the water for ten to twenty seconds. Drain the noodles and move to serving plate.

5. Pour the sauce over the noodles. Serve with lime wedges.

Yield: Servings 1–2

CLEAR NOODLES WITH BAKED SHRIMP

Ingredients:

- ¼ cup chopped cilantro

- 1 7-ounce package rice noodles

- 1 medium onion, thinly cut

- 1 tablespoon soy or fish sauce Sesame oil to taste

- 1 tablespoon vegetable oil

- 1 teaspoon sugar

- 2 cloves garlic, chopped

- 20–30 black peppercorns

- 6 big shrimp, shell on, washed and patted dry

Directions:

1. Soak the noodles in hot water until soft, approximately ten minutes. Drain and save for later.

2. Using a mortar and pestle or a food processor, meticulously mix the garlic, cilantro, and peppercorns.

3. Put in the vegetable oil to a wok or big frying pan using low heat. Put in the garlic mixture and stir-fry for a minute. Put in the cut onion and carry on cooking until the onion is soft, then remove the heat.

4. Put in the sugar, soy sauce, and a few drops of sesame oil to the wok; stir until blended. Put in the noodles and toss to coat. Pour the noodle mixture into an ovenproof baking dish. Put the whole shrimp on top of the noodles, cover the dish, and bake for about twenty minutes in a 400-degree oven. Serve instantly.

Yield: Servings 2

CURRIED RICE NOODLES WITH TOFU AND EGG
Ingredients:

- ½ of a 7-ounce package rice noodles

- ½ teaspoon ground coriander

- ½ teaspoon ground cumin

- 1 cup bean sprouts

- 1 cup coconut milk

- 1 cup cubed extra-firm tofu

- 1 green onion, trimmed and thinly cut

- 1 hard-boiled egg, cut

- 1 tablespoon Red Curry Paste (Page 17)

- 1 teaspoon curry powder

- 2 tablespoons chopped cilantro

- 2 tablespoons fish sauce

- 2 tablespoons minced shallots

- 2 tablespoons sugar

- 2–3 cups water

Directions:

1. In a small container, meticulously mix the coriander, cumin, curry powder, and curry paste.

2. Pour the coconut milk into a moderate-sized deep cooking pan. Mix in the curry paste mixture and place on moderate heat. Heat to a simmer and cook for approximately five minutes or until a slim layer of yellow oil starts to make on the surface of the sauce.

3. Mix in 2 cups of the water, the shallots, sugar, and fish sauce. Return the sauce to a simmer and allow to cook thirty minutes, stirring once in a while and putting in extra water if required.
4. In the meantime, soak the noodles in hot water for about ten minutes or until tender.

5. To serve, mound the noodles into serving bowls. Top the noodles with the cut egg, tofu, and bean sprouts. Ladle some of the curry sauce over top. Drizzle with green onion slices and chopped cilantro.

Yield: Servings 2 as a main course or 4 as an appetizer.

FIRE NOODLES

Ingredients:

- fifteen–20 (or to taste) Thai bird chilies, stemmed and seeded 1 pound presliced
- fresh rice noodles (available at Asian grocery stores and on the Internet)

- 2 tablespoons vegetable oil

- 2 whole boneless, skinless chicken breasts, cut into bite-sized pieces

- 2 tablespoons fish sauce

- 2 tablespoons sweet black soy sauce

- 1 tablespoon oyster sauce

- 1 teaspoon white pepper

- 1½ tablespoons sugar

- 1 (8-ounce) can bamboo shoots, drained 1½ cups loose-packed basil and/or mint 5–10
- (or to taste) cloves
- garlic

Directions:

1. Put the chilies and garlic cloves in a food processor and pulse until meticulously mashed together; set aside.

2. Bring a kettle of water to its boiling point. Put the noodles in a big colander and pour the hot water over them. Cautiously unfold and separate the noodles; set aside.

3. Heat the oil in a wok or big frying pan on moderate to high heat. When it is fairly hot, cautiously put in the reserved chili-garlic mixture and stir-fry for fifteen seconds to release the aromas.

4. Increase the heat to high, put in the chicken, and stir-fry until it starts to lose its color, approximately half a minute.

5. Mix in the fish sauce, soy sauce, oyster sauce, white pepper, and sugar.

6. Put in the noodles and continue to stir-fry for half a minute, tossing them with the other ingredients.

7. Put in the bamboo shoots and cook for one more minute.

8. Remove the heat and put in the basil.

Yield: Servings 4–6

FLOWERED LIME NOODLES

Ingredients:

- 1 tablespoon salted butter

- 2–3 tablespoons lime juice

- 4 ounces grated Parmesan cheese

- 8 ounces angel hair pasta

- Black pepper

- Lime slices

- Rose petals or other organic edible flowers

Directions:

1. Bring a big pot of water to its boiling point using high heat. Put in pasta and cook in accordance with package instructions; drain.

2. Toss the pasta with butter, lime juice, and parmesan.

3. To serve, top with rose or flower petals and lime slices. Pass black pepper at the table.

Yield: Servings 4

PAD THAI

Ingredients:

- ¼ cup brown sugar

- ¼ cup chopped chives

- ¼ cup fish sauce

- ½ cup chopped roasted peanuts

- ½ cup cooked salad shrimp

- 1 cup bean sprouts

- 1 medium egg, beaten

- 2 tablespoons chopped shallots

- 2 tablespoons vegetable oil

- 5–6 cloves garlic, finely chopped

- 6–8 teaspoons Tamarind Concentrate (Page 20)

- 8 ounces rice noodles

Garnish:

- ½ cup bean sprouts

- ½ cup chopped chives

- ½ cup crudely ground roasted peanuts

- 1 lime cut into wedges

- 1 tablespoon fish sauce

- 1 tablespoon lime juice

- 1 tablespoon <u>Tamarind Concentrate (Page 20)</u>

Directions:

1. Soak the noodles in water at room temperature for thirty minutes or until tender. Drain and save for later.

2. Heat the vegetable oil in a wok or frying pan on moderate to high heat. Put in the garlic and shallots, and for a short period of time stir-fry until they start to change color.

3. Put in the reserved noodles and all the rest of the ingredients except the egg and the bean sprouts, and stir-fry until hot.

4. While continuously stirring, slowly sprinkle in the beaten egg.

5. Put in the bean sprouts and cook for no more than another half a minute.

6. In a small container combine all of the decorate ingredients apart from the lime wedges.

7. To serve, position the Pad Thai on a serving platter. Top with the decorate and surround with lime wedges.

Yield: Servings 2–4

PANANG MUSSELS AND NOODLES

Ingredients:

- ¼ cup white wine

- 1 medium onion, chopped

- 1 pound Asian egg noodles

- 1 pound mussels, washed and debearded

- 1 teaspoon <u>Black Bean Paste (Page 10)</u>

- 2 cups chicken broth

- 2 tablespoons vegetable oil

- 6—8 stalks celery, chopped

Directions:

1. Bring a big pot of water to its boiling point using high heat. Put in the noodles and cook until firm to the bite. Wash the noodles under cold water and save for later.

2. Heat the oil in a big sauté pan on moderate heat. Put in the Black Bean Paste, onion, and celery, and sauté for five minutes.

3. Put in the wine and chicken broth, and bring to its boiling point.

4. Put in the mussels and decrease the heat to low; cover and steam for five minutes.

5. To serve, split the noodles between 4 soup plates. Split the mussels between the plates (discarding any that have not opened) and pour the broth over the top.

Yield: Servings 4

PAN–FRIED NOODLES

Ingredients:

- ¼ cup minced chives

- ¾ pound fresh lo mein noodles or angel hair pasta

- 2 tablespoons (or to taste) prepared chili-garlic paste

- 3 tablespoons vegetable oil, divided

- Salt to taste

Directions:

1. Boil the noodles in a big pot for no more than two to three minutes. Drain, wash under cold water, and drain once more.

2. Put in the chives, chili paste, 1 tablespoon of the oil, and salt to the noodles; toss to coat, and tweak seasonings.

3. In a heavy-bottomed 10-inch frying pan, heat the rest of the oil on moderate to high heat. When it is hot, put in the noodle mixture, spreading uniformly. Push the noodles into the pan using the back of a spatula. Cook for roughly two minutes.

Decrease the heat and carry on cooking until the noodles are well browned. Flip the noodles over in 1 piece. Carry on cooking until browned, putting in additional oil if required.

4. To serve, chop the noodles into wedges.

Yield: Servings 6–8

POACHED CHICKEN BREAST WITH PEANUT SAUCE AND NOODLES

Ingredients:

- ¼ cup chicken stock

- ¼ cup lime juice

- ¼ cup half-and-half

- 1 cup crispy peanut butter

- 1 pound Chinese egg noodles (mein)

- 1 pound snow peas, trimmed and blanched

- 1 tablespoon peanut oil

- 1 tablespoon sesame oil

- 1½ cups coconut milk

- 2 tablespoons fish sauce

- 2 teaspoons brown sugar

- 3 whole boneless, skinless chicken breasts, halved and poached

- 4 cloves garlic, minced

6–8 green onions, trimmed and thinly
- cut Salt and pepper
- to taste

Directions:

1. Mix the peanut butter, coconut milk, fish sauce, lime juice, brown sugar, garlic, salt, and pepper in a small deep cooking pan using low heat. Cook until the desired smoothness is achieved and thick, stirring regularly.

2. Move to a blender and purée.

3. Put in the chicken stock and half-and-half, and blend; set aside.

4. Bring a big pot of water to its boiling point. Put in the noodles and cook until firm to the bite. Drain, wash under cold water, and drain once more.

5. Toss the noodles with the peanut and sesame oils.

6. To serve, place some pasta in the center of each serving plate. Ladle some of the peanut sauce over the pasta. Slice each chicken breast on the diagonal. Move 1 cut breast to the top of each portion of

noodles. Ladle some additional peanut sauce over the chicken. Surround the noodles with the snow peas. Decorate using the cut green onions.

Yield: Servings 6

RICE STICK NOODLES WITH CHICKEN AND VEGETABLES

Ingredients:
Noodles:

- 1 tablespoon sweet black soy sauce

- 2 tablespoons vegetable oil

- 8 ounces rice stick noodles

Chicken and vegetables:

- ¼ cup chicken broth

- ¼– cup cut green onions

- ¼ pound broccoli, chopped

- ½ teaspoon Tabasco

- 1 big whole boneless, skinless chicken breast, cut into bite-sized strips

- 1 cup bean sprouts

- 1 small onion, finely cut

- 1 small red bell pepper, seeded and slice into strips

- 1 tablespoon cornstarch mixed with

- 1 tablespoon water

- 1¼ cups cut Japanese eggplant

- 2 tablespoons fish sauce

- 2 tablespoons vegetable oil

- 2 tablespoons Yellow Bean Sauce (Page 24)

- 3 tablespoons brown sugar

- 4 cloves garlic, chopped

Yield: Servings 2–4

NOODLES:

1. Soak the noodles in warm water for fifteen minutes or until soft; drain.

2. Put a wok on moderate to high heat and put in the vegetable oil. Once the oil is hot, put in the noodles and stir-fry vigorously until they are thoroughly heated, approximately 45 seconds to one minute.

3. Put in the soy sauce and continue to stir-fry for 1 more minute.

4. Put the noodles on a serving platter, covered in foil, in a warm oven until ready to serve.

CHICKEN AND VEGETABLES:

1. Put a wok on moderate to high heat and put in the vegetable oil. Once the oil is hot, put in the garlic and stir-fry for a short period of time to release its aroma.

2. Put in the chicken and cook until it begins to become opaque.

3. Put in the broccoli and stir-fry for half a minute.

4. Put in the onion and eggplant and stir-fry for a couple of minutes.

5. Put in the Tabasco, fish sauce, yellow bean sauce, and sugar. Stir-fry for a minute.

6. Put in the broth, cornstarch mixture, bean sprouts, green onions, and red bell pepper; cook until vegetables are soft-crisp.

7. To serve, ladle the chicken and vegetable mixture over the reserved noodles.

SESAME NOODLES WITH VEGGIES

Ingredients:

- 1 red bell pepper, seeded and slice into strips
- 1 tablespoon sesame oil
- 2 cloves garlic, minced
- 2 cups broccoli, cut into bite-sized pieces
- 2 tablespoons vegetable oil
- 2 tablespoons water
- 2–3 tablespoons prepared chili sauce
- 2–3 tablespoons soy sauce
- 3 tablespoons sesame seeds
- 4 ounces tofu, cut into bitesized cubes
- 8 ounces egg noodles

Directions:

1. Heat the oil in a big Sauté pan or wok on moderate heat. Put in the garlic and sauté until golden, roughly two minutes.

2. Put in the broccoli and red bell pepper, and stir-fry for two to three minutes. Put in the water, cover, and let the vegetables steam until soft, roughly five minutes.

3. Bring a big pot of water to boil. Put in the noodles and cook until firm to the bite; drain.

4. While the noodles are cooking, put in the rest of the ingredients to the broccoli mixture. Turn off the heat, put in the noodles, and toss to blend.

Yield: Servings 2–4

SPICY EGG NOODLES WITH SLICED PORK

Ingredients:

- ½ teaspoon vegetable oil

- 1 cup bean sprouts

- 1 package fresh angel hair pasta

- 1 small Barbecued Pork

- 1 small cabbage, shredded

- 2 scallions, trimmed and thinly cut

- 2 tablespoons fish sauce

- 2 tablespoons sugar

- 2 teaspoons chopped cilantro

- 2 teaspoons ground dried red chili pepper (or to taste)

- 4 tablespoons minced garlic

- 4–6 tablespoons rice vinegar

- Freshly ground black pepper to taste

- <u>Tenderloin</u>, thinly cut

Directions:

1. Bring a big pot of water to its boiling point using high heat. Put in the cabbage and blanch about half a minute. Using a slotted spoon, remove the cabbage from the boiling water; set aside.

2. Allow the water return to boiling. Put in the bean sprouts and blanch for ten seconds. Using a slotted spoon, remove the sprouts from the water; set aside.

3. Return the water to boiling. Put in the fresh angel hair pasta and cook in accordance with package directions. Drain the pasta and place it in a big mixing container.

4. In a small sauté pan, heat the vegetable oil on moderate heat. Put in the garlic and sauté until golden. Turn off the heat. Mix in the fish sauce, sugar, rice vinegar, and dried chili pepper.

5. Pour the sauce over the pasta and toss to coat.

6. To serve, split the cabbage and the bean sprouts into 2 to 4 portions and place in the middle of serving plates. Split the

noodles into 2 to 4 portions and place over the cabbage and sprouts. Split the pork slices over the noodles. Grind black pepper to taste over the noodles and top with the cut scallions and chopped cilantro.

Yield: Servings 2 as a main course or 4 as an appetizer.

THAI NOODLES WITH CHICKEN AND PORK

Ingredients:

For the sauce:

- ¼ teaspoon white pepper

- ½ cup peanut butter

- ½ cup soy sauce

- 1 teaspoon hot chili oil

- 1 teaspoon minced garlic

- 3 tablespoons honey

- 3 tablespoons sesame oil

For the noodles:

- ½ pound boneless pork tenderloin, cut into fine strips

- ½ pound boneless, skinless chicken breast, cut thin

- ½ teaspoon minced garlic

- 1 big yellow onion, diced

- 1 pound dry flat Asian noodles

- 1 tablespoon vegetable oil

- 1 teaspoon sesame oil

- 6 ounces salad shrimp

- 6–8 green onions, trimmed, white portions cut, green portions julienned

Directions:

1. Put all of the sauce ingredients in a blender and pulse until smooth; set aside.

2. Bring a big pot of water to boil using high heat. Prepare the noodles in accordance with package directions, drain, and mix in the sauce mixture, saving for later ¼ cup; set aside.

3. Heat the oils in a big sautée pan using high heat. Put in the garlic and sautée for a short period of time.

4. Put in the chicken, pork, and onion, and sauté for five to six minutes or until the meats are thoroughly cooked.

5. Put in the white portion of the green onion and the shrimp and sautée for two more minutes.

6. Put in the green parts of the onions and the rest of the sauce, stirring until everything is thoroughly coated.

7. To serve, put the noodles on a big platter and top with the meat sautée. Pass additional hot chili oil separately.

Yield: Servings 4

BASIC STICKY RICE

Ingredients:

- 1 cup glutinous rice

- Water

Directions:

1. Put the rice in a container, completely cover it with water, and allow to soak overnight. Drain before you use.

2. Coat a steamer basket or colander with moistened cheesecloth. (This prevents the grains of rice from falling through the holes in the colander.)

3. Spread the rice over the cheesecloth as uniformly as you can.

4. Bring a pan of water with a cover to a rolling boil. Put the basket over the boiling water, ensuring that the bottom of it doesn't come in contact with the water. Cover firmly and allow to steam for about twenty-five minutes.

Yield: Servings 2–4

BASIC WHITE RICE

Ingredients:

- 1 cup long-grain rice (such as Jasmine)

- 2 cups water

Directions:

1. Put the rice in a colander and run under cool water.
2. Put the rice and the water in a moderate-sized pot. Stir for a short period of time. Bring to a rolling boil on moderate to high heat. Decrease the heat to low, cover, and simmer for eighteen to twenty minutes.

3. Take away the rice from the heat, keeping it covered, and allow it to rest for minimum ten minutes.

4. Fluff the rice just before you serve.

Yield: Servings 2–4

CHICKEN FRIED RICE

Ingredients:

- ¼ cup chicken stock

- ¼ cup dry sherry

- ¼ cup fish sauce

- ½ medium head Chinese cabbage, crudely chopped 1
- cup shredded, cooked chicken

- 1 cup snow peas, trimmed and slice into bite-sized pieces

- 1 medium onion, cut

- 1 tablespoon minced garlic

- 1 tablespoon minced ginger

- 1 tablespoon vegetable oil

- 2 eggs, beaten

- 3 cups cooked long-grain white rice

Directions:

1. In a big frying pan or wok, heat the oil on moderate to low heat. Put in the garlic, ginger, and onion, and stir-fry for five minutes or until the onion becomes translucent.

2. Put in the cabbage, raise the heat to moderate, and stir-fry for about ten minutes.

3. Put in the rice and stir-fry for a couple of minutes.

4. Mix the fish sauce, sherry, and stock in a small container; put into the wok and stir until blended.

5. Put in the snow peas and chicken; stir-fry for a couple of minutes more.

6. Move the rice to the sides of the wok, making a hole in the center. Pour the eggs into the hole and cook for approximately 1 minute, stirring the eggs using a fork. Fold the cooked eggs into the fried rice.

Yield: Servings 4–6

CURRIED RICE

Ingredients:

- ¼ cup golden raisins (regular raisins can be substituted)

- ½ cup finely chopped onion

- 1 teaspoon curry powder

- 1½ cups long-grained rice

- 2 tablespoons vegetable oil

- 2 teaspoons Mango Chutney (Page 220)

- 2¾ cups vegetable stock

- Salt to taste

Directions:

1. In a moderate-sized-sized pot, heat the oil on moderate heat. Put in the onions and sautée. for a couple of minutes, until the onions are tender but not browned.

2. Put in the rice and continue to sautée. for another two minutes. Put in the curry powder and sauté for 1 more minute.

3. Pour in the vegetable stock and sprinkle with salt. Bring to its boiling point, then decrease the heat and cover. Simmer the rice for fifteen to twenty minutes, stirring once in a while.

4. Put in the raisins and the chutney. Continue to simmer for another five minutes or until soft.

Yield: Servings 4–6

DILL RICE

Ingredients:

- 1 cup long-grained rice (such as Jasmine)

  1 green chili pepper, seeded and
- minced 1½ cups
- water

- 2 green cardamom pods

- 2 tablespoons vegetable oil

- 4 tablespoons chopped fresh dill

- Salt

Directions:

1. In a moderate-sized-sized pot, heat the vegetable oil on moderate heat. Put in the cardamom pods and sauté for a minute. Put in the chili and sautée. for a short period of time. Mix in the salt and the dill and cook for another two to three minutes. Put in the rice and sauté for 3 more minutes.

2. Mix in the water and bring the mixture to its boiling point. Decrease the heat, cover, and simmer for twenty to twenty-five minutes or until the liquid has been absorbed.

3. Take away the cardamom pods and fluff the rice before you serve.

Yield: Servings 2–4

FAR EAST FRIED RICE

Ingredients:

- ¼ cup chopped mint or cilantro leaves

- ¼ cup roasted peanuts, chopped

- 1 bunch green onions, trimmed and thinly cut

- 1 teaspoon dried red chili pepper flakes 1½ tablespoons rice vinegar

- 2 big carrots, peeled and crudely shredded

- 2 cups bean sprouts, trimmed if required

- 2 eggs, beaten

- 2 tablespoons fish sauce

- 2 tablespoons minced garlic

- 2 tablespoons sugar

- 2½ tablespoons vegetable oil

- 5 cups day-old long-grain white rice, clumps broken up

Directions:

1. Mix the fish sauce, rice vinegar, and sugar in a small container; set aside.

2. In a wok or big frying pan, heat the oil on moderate to high heat. Put in the eggs and stir-fry until scrambled.

3. Put in the green onions, garlic, and pepper flakes and continue to stir-fry for fifteen seconds or until aromatic.

4. Put in the carrots and bean sprouts; stir-fry until the carrots start to tenderize, approximately 2 minutes.

5. Put in the rice and cook for two to three minutes or until thoroughly heated.

6. Mix in the fish sauce mixture and put in the fried rice, tossing until uniformly coated.

7. To serve, decorate the rice with chopped mint, or cilantro, and chopped peanuts.

Yield: Servings 4–6

FLAVORFUL STEAMED RICE

Ingredients:

- ¼ cup chicken or vegetable broth

- ½ cup finely chopped cilantro

- ¾ cup long-grained rice

- 1 tablespoon minced gingerroot

- 1 teaspoon fish sauce

- 1 teaspoon salt

- 2 cloves garlic, minced

- 2 green onions, trimmed and thinly cut

- 2 teaspoons lime juice

Directions:

1. Bring a pot of water to a rolling boil. Put in the rice, allow the water to return to its boiling point, and cook for about ten minutes. Drain in a sieve, wash, and save for later. (Leave the rice in the sieve.)

2. Put in 1 inch of water to the pot and bring to its boiling point. Set the sieve over the

boiling water, cover it using a clean kitchen towel and a lid, and allow to steam for approximately twenty minutes. (Check once in a while, putting in more water if required.)

3. Mash together the garlic and the salt to make a paste.

4. In a big container, mix the garlic paste, broth, gingerroot, green onions, lime juice, and fish sauce.

5. Put in the steamed rice and toss until well blended. Allow to cool to room temperature.

6. Mix the cilantro into the rice.

Yield: Servings 2–4

FRAGRANT BROWN RICE

Ingredients:

- 1 cups brown rice (white rice can be substituted)

- 1 kaffir lime leaf or 2 (2-inch-long, -½inch-wide) pieces of lime zest

- 1 medium carrot, peeled and julienned

- 1 tablespoon finely chopped gingerroot

- 1 tablespoon lime juice

- 1½ stalks celery, trimmed and thinly cut 2 garlic cloves,
- minced

- 2 red chili peppers, seeded and minced

- 2 tablespoons vegetable oil

- 4 green onions, trimmed and thinly cut 4½–5½ cups vegetable
- stock

- Salt and freshly ground pepper to taste

Directions:

1. In a moderate-sized to big deep cooking pan, heat the vegetable oil on medium. Put in the garlic and green onions, and cook for a couple of minutes. Put in the celery, carrots, chilies, and ginger, and cook for another two minutes.

2. Put in the rice and stir until well blended. Put in half of the vegetable stock, the kaffir lime leaf, lime juice, and salt and pepper. Bring to its boiling point; decrease the heat and simmer, uncovered, for fifty minutes, putting in additional stock as required.

Yield: Servings 4–6

FRAGRANT WHITE RICE

Ingredients:

- 1 stalk lemongrass, cut into thin rings (inner soft potion only)

- 10 fresh curry leaves

- 1¼ cups coconut milk

- 1¾ cups water

- 2 mace blades

- 2 tablespoons vegetable oil

- 2½ cups Jasmine rice

- 6 cloves

- Salt and freshly ground pepper to taste Zest of ½ kaffir lime

Directions:

1. In a moderate-sized-large deep cooking pan, heat the oil on medium. Put in the curry leaves and sautée. until you can start to smell the aroma. Put in the lime zest and the

rest of the spices and sautée. for another two to three minutes, stirring continuously.

2. Put in the rice to the pot and stir until blended with the spice mixture. Put in the water, coconut milk, and salt and pepper. Bring to its boiling point; reduce heat, cover, and simmer for fifteen to twenty minutes or until the liquids have been absorbed. Adjust seasoning.

Yield: Servings 6–8

FRIED RICE WITH CHINESE OLIVES

Ingredients:

- ½ cup ground pork or chicken

- 10 Chinese olives, pitted and chopped

- 3 cloves garlic, minced

- 3 cups day-old cooked rice Fish sauce (not necessary)

- 3 tablespoons vegetable oil

- Chopped cilantro

- Cucumber slices

- Hot sauce

- Lime wedges

Directions:

1. Heat the oil in a wok or big frying pan on medium. Put in the garlic and stir-fry for a short period of time. Put in the pork and olives. Stir-fry until the pork is thoroughly cooked and any juices that have collected have cooked off.

2. Put in the rice, breaking up any clumps, and stir-fry until the rice Is hot. Adjust the saltiness with a small amount of fish sauce if required.

3. Serve accompanied by cucumber slices, lime wedges, chopped cilantro, and hot sauce.

Yield: Servings 2–3

FRIED RICE WITH PINEAPPLE AND SHRIMP

Ingredients:

- ½ teaspoon curry powder

- ½ teaspoon shrimp paste

- ½ teaspoon turmeric

- 1 cup finely chopped onion

- 1 ripe whole pineapple

- 2 garlic cloves, thoroughly minced 10 ounces peeled shrimp, deveined and slice into ½-inch pieces

- 2¼ cups day-old, cooked Jasmine or other long grained rice

- 4 tablespoons vegetable oil

- Salt to taste

- Sugar to taste

Directions:

1. To prepare the pineapple, cut it in half along the length, leaving the leaves undamaged on 1 side. Scoop out the pineapple flesh of both

halves, leaving a ½-inch edge on the half with the leaves. Reserve the hollowed-out half to use as a serving container. Dice the pineapple fruit and save for later.

2. Preheat your oven to 350 degrees.

3. In a wok or heavy sauté pan, heat the oil on medium. Put in the onion and garlic, and sauté until the onion is translucent. Using a slotted spoon, remove the onions and garlic from the wok and save for later.

4. Put in the shrimp and sauté roughly one minute; remove and save for later.

5. Put in the turmeric, curry powder, and shrimp paste to the wok; stir-fry for a short period of time. Put in the rice and stir-fry for two to three minutes. Put in the pineapple and carry on cooking. Put in the reserved shrimp, onions, and garlic. Season to taste with salt and sugar.

6. Mound the fried rice into the pineapple "serving container." Put the pineapple on a baking sheet and bake for roughly ten minutes. Serve instantly.

Yield: Servings 2–4

FRIED RICE WITH TOMATOES

Ingredients:

- 1 clove garlic, minced

- 1 green onion, trimmed and cut

- 1 medium onion, slivered

- 1 teaspoon fish sauce

- 1 teaspoon ground white pepper

- 1 teaspoon sugar

- 1 tomato, cut into 8–10 wedges

- 1 whole boneless, skinless chicken breast, cut into bitesized pieces

- 2 eggs

- 2 teaspoons soy sauce

- 3 tablespoons vegetable oil

- 4 cups cooked rice

Directions:

1. In a big frying pan or wok, heat the vegetable oil on moderate to high. Put in the chicken pieces and the garlic, and stir-fry one minute.

2. Put in the onion and continue to stir-fry for another minute.

3. Break in the eggs, stirring thoroughly.

4. Mix in all the rest of the ingredients; stir-fry for two more minutes.

5. Serve instantly.

Yield: Servings 2–4

GINGER RICE

Ingredients:

- 1 (½-inch) piece of gingerroot, peeled and thinly cut

- 1 red chili pepper, seeded and minced

- 1 stalk lemongrass, cut into rings (soft inner portion only)

- 1½ cups long-grained rice

- 2 tablespoons vegetable oil

- 2¾ cups water

- 2—3 green onions, cut into rings

- Juice of ½ lime

- Pinch of brown sugar

- Pinch of salt

Directions:

1. In a moderate-sized-sized pot, heat the oil on moderate heat. Put in the gingerroot, lemongrass, green onions,

and chili pepper; sautée. for two to three minutes.

2. Put in the rice, brown sugar, salt, and lime juice, and continue to sautée. for another two minutes. Put in the water to the pot and bring to its boiling point.

3. Reduce the heat, cover with a tight-fitting lid, and simmer for fifteen to twenty minutes, until the liquid is absorbed.

Yield: Servings 4–6

LEMON RICE

Ingredients:

- ¼ cup cashew nuts, soaked in cold water for five minutes

- ¼ teaspoon mustard seed

- ½ teaspoon turmeric

- 1 cup basmati rice, soaked in cold water for thirty minutes

- 1 cups water Pinch of salt

- 1 green chili pepper, seeded and minced

- 1 tablespoon vegetable oil

- 8 fresh curry leaves

- Juice of ½ lemon

Directions:

1. In a moderate-sized-sized pan, bring the water to its boiling point. Put in the salt, rice, and turmeric; reduce heat, cover, and simmer for about ten minutes. (At the end of the ten minutes, the rice will have

absorbed all of the liquid.) Turn off the heat and allow to cool.

2. In a wok, heat the oil and stir-fry the chili pepper. Put in the nuts, mustard seed, and curry leaves; carry on cooking for another half a minute. Mix in the lemon juice. Put in the cooled rice to the wok and toss until heated.

Yield: Servings 2–4

SHRIMP RICE

Ingredients:

- 1 ¾cups long-grained rice

- 1 medium to big onion, finely chopped

- 1 quart water

- 1 stalk lemongrass, halved and crushed (inner white potion only)

- 1 tablespoon lime juice

- 2 cloves garlic, finely chopped

- 2 red chili peppers, seeded, veined, and thoroughly minced

- 4 tablespoons fish sauce

- 5 tablespoons dried shrimp, soaked in cold water for about ten minutes

- 5 tablespoons vegetable oil

- Salt to taste

Directions:

1. Make a shrimp paste by combining the dried shrimp, chili peppers, onion, and garlic in a blender or food processor and processing until the desired smoothness is achieved.

2. In a moderate-sized-sized deep cooking pan, warm the oil on moderate heat. Put in the shrimp paste and cook for three to four minutes, stirring continuously.

3. Put in the fish sauce, lime juice, and salt to the paste and stir until well mixed; set aside.

4. Pour the rice into a big pot and put the lemongrass on top. Put in the water and bring to its boiling point; reduce heat, cover, and simmer for fifteen minutes.

5. Take away the lemongrass stalk and mix in the shrimp paste. Carry on cooking for five to ten minutes or until the rice is done.

Yield: Servings 4–6

SWEET-SPICED FRIED RICE

Ingredients:

- ½ teaspoon mace

- 1 (1-inch) cinnamon stick

- 1 bay leaf

- 1 tablespoon brown sugar

- 1½ cups long-grained rice (such as Jasmine)

- 2¼ cups water

- 3 cloves

- 3 tablespoons vegetable oil ½
- onion, cut into rings Salt

Directions:

1. Soak the rice in cold water for about twenty minutes.

2. In the meantime, heat the oil in a moderate-sized pot on moderate heat. Put in the onions and sauté until golden, roughly ten to fifteen minutes.

3. Put in the spices and sauté for another two minutes. Drizzle the brown sugar over the onlon mixture and caramelize for one to two minutes, stirring continuously. Put in the rice and sautée. for another three minutes, stirring continuously.

4. Put in the salt and the water to the pot and bring to its boiling point. Decrease the heat, cover, and simmer until the rice is soft, roughly ten to fifteen minutes.

5. Take away the cinnamon stick and cloves before you serve.

Yield: Approximately 4 cups

VEGETARIAN FRIED RICE

Ingredients:

- ½ cup finely diced onion

- ½ cup vegetable stock

- ½ teaspoon brown sugar

- ½ teaspoon ground turmeric

- 1 tablespoon finely chopped fresh gingerroot

- 2 garlic cloves, finely chopped

- 2 medium carrots, peeled and julienned into 1-inch pieces

- 2 red chili peppers, seeded, veined, and thinly cut

- 2 stalks of celery, cut

- 2 tablespoons vegetarian "oyster" sauce

- 3 cups day-old long-grained rice

- 3 tablespoons soy sauce

- 3 tablespoons vegetable oil, divided

- 4 scallions, cut

- 7 ounces green beans, trimmed and slice into 1-inch pieces

- 9 ounces tomatoes, peeled, seeded, and diced

- Grated zest and juice of ½ of a lime
- Salt and freshly ground pepper to
- taste

Directions:

1. In a wok or big sauté pan, heat 2 tablespoons of the vegetable oil on moderate to high heat. Put in the rice and stir-fry for two to three minutes. Take away the rice from the wok and save for later.

2. Put in the remaining tablespoon of oil to the wok. Put in the onion, garlic, and ginger; sauté for a minute.

3. Put in the chilies, scallions, green beans, carrots, and celery; stir-fry for about three minutes.

4. Put in the stock and bring to its boiling point; decrease the heat and simmer for five minutes.

5. Put in the tomatoes and simmer for another two minutes.

6. Put in the "oyster" and soy sauces and turmeric. Sprinkle salt and pepper to taste.

7. Mix in the lime zest, lime juice, brown sugar, and rice. Mix until blended.

Yield: Servings 4–

BANANA COCONUT SOUP

Ingredients:

- 1 cinnamon stick

- 1 tablespoon lemon juice

- 2 tablespoons minced gingerroot

- 4 cups banana slices, plus extra for decoration

- 4 cups canned coconut milk

- Salt to taste

Directions:

1. In a big deep cooking pan, bring the coconut milk to its boiling point. Put in the banana, ginger, cinnamon stick, lemon juice, and a pinch of salt. Decrease the heat and simmer for ten to fifteen minutes or until the banana is very tender.

2. Take away the cinnamon stick and let cool slightly.

3. Using a handheld blender (or a blender or food processor), purée the soup until the desired smoothness is achieved.

4. Serve the soup in preheated bowls, decorated with banana slices and coconut.

Yield: Servings 6–8

BANANAS POACHED IN COCONUT MILK

Ingredients:

- ¼ teaspoon salt

- 1 cup sugar

- 2–3 small, slightly green bananas

- 4 cups coconut milk

Directions:

1. Peel the bananas and slice them in half along the length.

2. Pour the coconut milk into a pan big enough to hold the bananas laid flat in a single layer. Put in the sugar and salt and bring to its boiling point.

3. Reduce the heat, put in the bananas, and simmer until the bananas are just warmed through, approximately 3 to five minutes.

4. Serve the bananas warm on small plates decorated with fresh coconut and pineapple wedges.

Yield: Servings 2–3

CITRUS FOOL

Ingredients:

- ½ cup heavy cream

- ½ cup orange, lime, or lemon juice

- 1 big egg, beaten

- 2 (3-inch-long, ½-inch wide) strips of citrus zest, minced

- 3 tablespoons sugar

- 3 tablespoons unsalted butter

Directions:

1. Put the juice in a small deep cooking pan. Over moderate to high heat, reduce the liquid by half.

2. Take away the pan from the heat and mix in the sugar and butter. Mix in the egg until well blended.

3. Return the pan to the burner and cook on medium-low heat for three to five minutes or until bubbles barely start to form.

4. Take away the pan from the heat and mix in the citrus zest. Put the pan in a container of ice and stir the mixture until it is cold.

5. In another container, whip the cream until firm. Fold the citrus mixture meticulously into the cream.

Yield: Servings 4

.

COCONUT CUSTARD

Ingredients:

- 1 (16-ounce) can coconut cream

- 3 tablespoons butter

- 6 big eggs, lightly beaten

- 1 cup fine granulated sugar

- Fresh tropical fruit (not necessary)

Directions:

1. In a large, heavy-bottomed deep cooking pan, mix together the coconut cream and the sugar.

2. Over moderate heat, cook and stir the mixture until the sugar is thoroughly blended.

3. Lower the heat to low and mix in the eggs. Cook while stirring once in a while, until the mixture is thick and coats the back of a spoon, approximately ten to twelve minutes.

4. Take away the pan from the heat and put in the butter. Stir until the butter is completely melted and blended.

5. Pour the custard into six 4-ounce custard cups. Put the cups in a baking pan. Pour boiling water into the baking pan until it comes midway up the sides of the custard cups.

6. Cautiously move the baking pan to a preheated 325-degree oven. Bake the custards for thirty to forty minutes until set. (The tip of a knife should come out clean when inserted into the middle of the custard.)

7. Serve warm or at room temperature. Decorate using chopped tropical fruit, if you wish.

Yield: Servings 6

COCONUT-PINEAPPLE SOUFFLÉ FOR 2

Ingredients:

- ½ cup (½-inch) cubes ladyfingers or sponge cake

- 1 egg yolk

- 2 egg whites

- 2 tablespoons dark rum

- 2 tablespoons finely chopped fresh pineapple

- 2 tablespoons sugar

- 2½ tablespoons grated sweetened coconut Lemon juice

- Softened butter for the molds

- Sugar for the molds

Directions:

1. Preheat your oven to 400 degrees.

2. Butter 2-¾ or 1-cup soufflée molds and then drizzle them with sugar. Place in your fridge the molds until ready to use.

3. Put the ladyfinger cubes in a small container. Pour the rum over the cubes and allow to soak for five minutes.

4. Squeeze the juice from the pineapple, saving both the pulp and 1 tablespoon of the juice.

5. In a small container, beat the egg yolk with the pineapple juice until very thick. Fold in the cake cubes, pineapple pulp, and coconut.

6. In another small container, beat the egg whites with a few drops of lemon juice until foamy. Slowly put in the 2 tablespoons of sugar, while continuing to beat until the whites are stiff and shiny.

7. Lightly fold the pineapple mixture into the egg whites.
8. Ladle the batter into the prepared molds and bake for eight to ten minutes or until puffy and mildly browned.

Yield: 2

CRISPY CREPES WITH FRESH FRUIT

Ingredients:

- ¼ cup shredded, unsweetened coconut 1 cup heavy cream

- 1 package frozen puff pastry sheets, thawed in accordance with package instructions

- 1 tablespoon unflavored rum or coconut-flavored rum

- 2 cups raspberries, blueberries, or other fresh fruit, the best 12 berries reserved for decoration

- 2 tablespoons confectioner's sugar, divided

Directions:

1. Preheat your oven to 400 degrees.

2. Put the puff pastry sheet on a work surface and slice into 12 equalsized pieces. Put the pastry pieces on a baking sheet.

3. Bake the pastry roughly ten minutes. Take out of the oven and use a sifter to shake a

small amount of the confectioner?s sugar over the puff pastry. Return to the oven and carry on baking for roughly five minutes or until golden. Put the puff pastry on a wire rack and let cool completely.

4. Put the berries in a food processor and for a short period of time process to make a rough purée.

5. Whip the cream with the rest of the confectioner's sugar until thick, but not firm. Mix in the coconut and the rum.

6. To serve, place 1 piece of puff pastry in the center of each serving plate, spoon some cream over the pastry, and then top with some purée. Put another pastry on top, decorate with some of the rest of the berries, any remaining juice from the purée, and a drizzle of confectioner's sugar.

FRESH ORANGES IN ROSE WATER

Ingredients:

- 1½ cups sugar

- 3 cups water

- 4–6 teaspoons rose water

- 8 oranges

Directions:

1. Peel and segment the oranges. Put them in a container, cover, and set aside in your fridge.

2. In a deep cooking pan, bring the water and the sugar to its boiling point over moderatehigh heat. Boil gently for fifteen to 20 or until the mixture becomes syrupy. Turn off the heat and mix in the rose water. Allow to cool to room temperature and then place in your fridge

3. To serve, place orange segments in individual dessert cups. Pour rose water syrup over the top.

Yield: Servings 6–8

LEMONGRASS CUSTARD

Ingredients:

- ½ cup suga

- 2 cups whole milk

- 2 stalks fresh lemongrass, finely chopped (soft inner portion only)

- 6 egg yolks

Directions:

1. Preheat your oven to 275 degrees.

2. In a moderate-sized-sized deep cooking pan, on moderate to high heat, bring the milk and the lemongrass to its boiling point. Lower the heat and simmer for five minutes. Cover the milk mixture, remove the heat, and allow it to sit for about ten minutes on the burner.

3. In a mixing container, beat the egg yolks with the sugar until thick.

4. Strain the milk mixture through a fine-mesh sieve, then slowly pour it into the egg yolks, whisking continuously.

5. Split the mixture between 6 small custard cups and put the cups in a high-sided baking or roasting pan. Put in warm water to the pan so that it reaches to roughly an inch below the top of the custard cups. Cover the pan firmly using foil.

6. Put the pan in your oven and bake for roughly twenty minutes or until the custards are set on the sides but still slightly wobbly in the middle.

Yield: Servings 6

MANGO FOOL

Ingredients:

- ¼ cup sugar

- 1 cup heavy cream

- 1 tablespoon confectioners' sugar

- 2 ripe mangoes, peeled and flesh cut from the pits 2 tablespoons lime juice

- Crystallized ginger (not necessary)

- Mint leaves (not necessary)

Directions:

1. Put the mangoes in a food processor with the lime juice and sugar. Puréee until the desired smoothness is achieved.

2. In a big container beat the heavy cream with the confectioners' sugar until firm.

3. Thoroughly fold the mango purée into the heavy cream.

4. Serve in goblets decorated with crystallized ginger or sprigs of mint, if you wish.

Yield: Servings 4–6

MANGO SAUCE OVER ICE CREAM

Ingredients:

- 1 banana, peeled and chopped

- 1 tablespoon brandy (not necessary)

- 2 mangoes, peeled, pitted, and diced

- 1 cup (or to taste) sugar

- Juice of 2 big limes (or to taste)

- Vanilla ice cream

Directions:

1. In a moderate-sized-sized deep cooking pan using low heat, simmer the mangoes, banana, sugar, and lime juice for thirty minutes, stirring regularly.

2. Put in the brandy and simmer 5 more minutes.

3. Turn off the heat and let cool slightly or to room temperature.

4. To serve, scoop ice cream into individual serving bowls. Ladle sauce over top.

Yield: 2 cups

PINEAPPLE RICE

Ingredients:

- ¼ cup sugar

- ½ cup short-grained rice

- 1 ripe pineapple

- 2 teaspoons chopped crystallized ginger, divided

- 3 tablespoons roasted cashew nuts, chopped
- Pinch of salt

- Zest and juice of 1 lemon

Directions:

1. Chop the pineapple in half along the length, leaving the leaves undamaged on 1 side. Scoop out the pineapple flesh of both halves, leaving a ½-inch edge on the half with the leaves. Dice the pineapple fruit from 1 half and purée the fruit from the other half in a food processor together with the sugar and salt; set aside.

2. Strain the fruit purée through a fine-mesh sieve into a measuring cup. Put in enough

water to make 1¾ cups. Move to a small deep cooking pan and bring to its boiling point on moderate to high heat.

3. Wash and drain the rice. Mix the rice into the pineapple purée. Mix in the lemon zest, lemon juice, and 1 teaspoon of the ginger. Bring to its boiling point; reduce heat, cover, and simmer until the liquid has been absorbed, approximately twenty minutes.
4. Combine the reserved pineapple cubes into the rice.

5. To serve, spoon the rice into the hollowed out pineapple that has the leaves. Decorate using the rest of the ginger and the roasted cashews.

Yield: Servings 4–6

PINEAPPLE-MANGO SHERBET

Ingredients:

- ½ cup plain yogurt

- 1 big orange, peeled and segmented

- 1 cup pineapple pieces

- 1 tablespoon lime zest

- 1 teaspoon orange-flavored liqueur (not necessary)

- 2 mangoes, peeled, pitted, and slice into 1-inch cubes

- 1 cup sugar

Directions:

1. Put the orange segments, mango cubes, and pineapple pieces on a baking sheet lined with waxed paper; store in your freezer for 30 to forty-five minutes or until just frozen.

2. Move the fruit to a food processor. Put in the lime zest and sugar, and pulse until well blended.

3. While the machine runs, add the yogurt and liqueur. Process for another three minutes or until the mixture is fluffy.

4. Pour the mixture into an 8" × 8" pan, cover using foil, and freeze overnight.

5. To serve, let the sherbet temper at room temperature for ten to fifteen minutes, then scoop into glass dishes.

Yield: Servings 4–6

PUMPKIN CUSTARD

Ingredients:

- 1 small cooking pumpkin

- 5 eggs

- 1 cup brown sugar

Directions:

1. With a small sharp knife, cautiously chop the top off of the pumpkin.
2. Using a spoon, remove and discard the seeds and most of the tender flesh; set the pumpkin aside.

3. In a moderate-sized-sized mixing container, whisk the eggs together. Mix in the brown sugar, salt, and coconut cream until well blended.

4. Pour the mixture into the pumpkin.

5. Put the pumpkin in a steamer and allow to steam for roughly twenty minutes or until the custard is set.

Yield: Servings 4

PUMPKIN SIMMERED IN COCONUT MILK

Ingredients:

- ½ cup coconut milk

- ½ teaspoon salt

- 1 cup water

- 2 cups fresh pumpkin meat cut into big julienned pieces (acorn squash is a good substitute)

- 1 cup brown sugar

Directions:

1. Place the water and the coconut milk in a moderate-sized pan using low heat. Put in the salt and half of the sugar; stir until well blended. Adjust the sweetness to your preference by put in more water or sugar if required.

2. Put in the julienned pumpkin to the pan and bring to its boiling point on moderate heat. Reduce to a simmer and cook until soft, approximately 5 to ten minutes depending

on both the texture of the pumpkin and your own preference.

3. The pumpkin may be served hot, warm, or cold.

Yield: Servings 4